HANDBO

Seashore

Written by

Camilla de la Bédoyère

Miles
Kelly

First published in 2011 by Miles Kelly Publishing Ltd
Harding's Barn, Bardfield End Green, Thaxted, Essex, CM6 3PX, UK

This edition printed in 2013

2 4 6 8 10 9 7 5 3 1

Publishing Director *Belinda Gallagher*
Creative Director *Jo Cowan*
Editor *Claire Philip*
Cover Designer *Jo Cowan*
Designer *Jo Cowan*
Image Manager *Liberty Newton*
Production Manager *Elizabeth Collins*
Reprographics *Stephan Davis, Thom Allaway*
The Wildlife Trusts Advisor *Adam Cormack*

ISBN 978-1-78209-168-4

Printed in China

British Library Cataloguing-in-Publication Data
A catalogue record for this book is available from the British Library

ACKNOWLEDGEMENTS

The publishers would like to thank Bridgette James and Mike Saunders for the artwork they contributed to this book. All artworks are by these artists unless otherwise stated. The following artworks are from The Miles Kelly Artwork Bank: Page 23, 29, 45, 49, 57, 77, 79, 81, 83, 85, 87, 89, 91, 93 & 95.

The publishers would like to thank the following sources for the use of their photographs:

Alamy 70 Marcos Veiga **Ardea** 7(tl) David Kilbey; 62 Duncan Usher **Cathy Miles** 8(cl), 20, 58 **dreamstime.com** 7(bc) Robdaniels **FLPA** cover Steve Trewhella; 7(cl) Sunset; 9(tr), 50 & 86 Gary K Smith; 9(cl), 42 & 94 Erica Olsen; 9(cr) Robert Canis; 12 Hugh Clark; 14, 40 & 54 D P Wilson; 16, 52 & 66 Steve Trewhella; 22 & 76 Flip De Nooyer/FN/Minden; 26 Richard Becker; 28 & 30 Tony Wharton; 64 Peter Verhoog/FN/Minden; 80 Steve Young; 82 Bill Baston; 88 Paul Hobson; 92 Michael Mährlein/Imagebroker **iStockphoto.com** 44 Frank Daugherty; 84 Liz Leyden **Nature Picture Library** 36 Laurie Campbell; 60 Christophe Courteau; 72 Kim Taylor **NHPA** 46 Bill Coster **Philip Wells** 6(cr), 7(tr), (cr); 48 **rspb-images.com** 38 Richard Revels **Shutterstock.com** 2, 3 & 96(b/g) oku; 4–11(b/g) T.Allendorf; paperclips (throughout) Kostia; 5(br) sevenke; 6(l) Cameramannz; 6(br) & 7(br) Stephen Aaron Rees; 7(bl) OneSmallSquare, (tc) Niels Quist; 8(tr) gabrisigno, (br) Bob Blanchard; 24 David Hughes; 32 Ron Rowan Photography; 34 Christopher Jones; 56 Lynsey Allan; 68 Jens Stolt; 74 vblinov; 78 John A. Anderson; 90 Arto Hakola **The Wildlife Trusts** 18 Chris Wood; 96 Andy Pearson **Tracey Wells** 5(tr)

Made with paper from a sustainable forest

www.mileskelly.net
info@mileskelly.net

www.factsforprojects.com

Contents

Checklist: Mark off your seashore sightings in the tick boxes above.

Foreword

Seashores represent an unexplored frontier, full of amazing wildlife for budding nature enthusiasts to discover.

Uncovering the secrets of the wide variety of creatures that live in these places is a joy. You'll be astonished at what you can find, and there is always something new to amaze. If you look beyond the usual seashore species, things can get really interesting.

This book should help you identify some of the incredible seashore species that can be found on British coasts. Many widespread varieties of coastal wildlife are included, as well as some rare finds that are really worth searching for.

Inside, there are over 40 species to spot and each is accurately presented and easy to find. There's also space for your own photos, sketches and notes. Instructions on seashore safety, beachcombing tips and descriptions of the different types of coastal environments give an insightful look into these important places.

For me, seashores are a world of colourful creatures with equally colourful lives. And here in the UK we have thousands of miles of coastline to explore – so get down to the seaside and experience the magic.

Nick Baker

Become a seashore detective

All detectives need to prepare before they go exploring, and that is especially true for seashore detectives. Seashores are full of exciting things to discover, but can be dangerous places.

Bustling with life, rock pools are full of fascinatng animals to discover

Equipment

Fill in the pages in this book with your notes and sketches. Use a ruler to measure your finds and a magnifying glass to see details. Take photographs where possible.

Checklist

- O wellington boots
- O pens and pencils
- O rubber and ruler
- O camera
- O magnifying glass
- O bottle of water
- O bucket and net
- O plastic bags (to store samples)
- O sun hat and sun cream on hot days
- O warm, waterproof clothing on cold days
- O watch to check the time

Safety warnings alert you to possible dangers

Before you go exploring, check these things:

- Is the weather forecast good? Seashores can be dangerous in very wet or windy weather.

- Do you know where you are going, and how to get back?

- You must have an adult nearby when you are exploring seashores.

- Research where you are going in case there are special things you should look out for.

Seashore safety

Our seashores are precious places that are home to many living things. The best seashore detectives follow The Wildlife Trusts' Seashore Code when they explore any coastal environment.

Watch out! Some seashore animals bite, sting or nip

SEASHORE CODE

- Don't paddle or throw things into rock pools.
- Put rocks back in the same place you found them, the same way up as they were.
- Be very gentle with animals. If you pick them up, return them carefully to their place.
- Don't take any living things away with you.
- Don't pull seaweed off the rocks.
- Don't try to kick or pull limpets off the rocks.
- Keep an eye on the tide so you don't get cut off.
- Don't get too close to the cliffs.
- Keep away from soft mud and quicksand.
- Wash your hands before you put your fingers in your mouth or eat anything.
- Beware of big waves, especially at a rocky coast.
- Don't frighten seabirds – give them some space!
- Always take your litter home with you.

Tide times

Always find out when high and low tide will be before you visit a beach, to make sure you won't get stranded when the tide comes in. Knowing when the beach is uncovered will also allow the best exploration – you are more likely to find lots of sea life at low tide.

Low tide (above) and high tide (below) at St Michael's Mount, Cornwall

Beachcombing

Searching beaches for objects to identify is called beachcombing. Here are some things you might find washed up on the seashore.

Sea potatoes These sea urchins are in the same animal family as starfish.

Cuttlefish bone This white, hard structure comes from a cuttlefish, a type of mollusc.

Carapace Empty crab shells are often dotted along the beach.

Whelk egg case These empty bundles are also known as 'sea wash balls' as sailors used to use them to wash themselves.

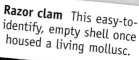

Razor clam This easy-to-identify, empty shell once housed a living mollusc.

Sun star This many-armed relative of the common starfish is easily recognisable.

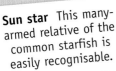

Mermaid's purse A rubbery mermaid's purse is the egg sac of a shark or dogfish.

Jellyfish This stranded sea creature belongs to the same animal family as sea anemones.

Seashore habitats

A seashore is a place where the sea or ocean meets the land. There are lots of different types of seashore, but they are all dynamic, exciting habitats (places where animals or plants survive).

Cliffs

These rocky seashore habitats are exposed to wind, waves, water spray, sunshine and rain — so they can be difficult places for living things to survive. Plants such as thrift, campion and lichen grow on cliffs.

This cliff-top provides a home for a colony of guillemots.

Rocky shores and rock pools

There are few places to burrow or hide on a rocky shore. However when the tide goes out, rock pools are great places to find wildlife. The best rock pools to investigate are the ones closest to the sea.

Look for anemones, crabs, small fish and seaweed in rock pools.

This turnstone is foraging for food on a sandy beach.

Sandy beaches and the strandline

These habitats are always changing, as wind and water continually shift the sand. Strandlines are the highest places the sea reaches on a beach. Look for marine debris that has been washed ashore after high tide.

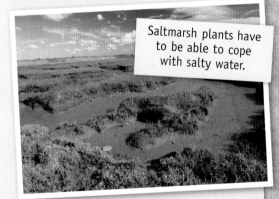

The yellow horned poppy is a resilient plant that can survive on pebbly shores.

Shingle beaches

Covered in multi-coloured pebbles, shingle beaches are tough places to live and grow. Some plants, such as sea kale and yellow horned poppies are hardy enough to survive the changeable conditions.

Dunes make good resting places for grey seals and their pups.

Dunes

Large dunes develop when the wind moves sand to a place where it can collect and build up. Dunes change and move because dry sand is easily blown to new places by the wind. These habitats support many animals and plants, such as lizards and orchids.

Saltmarshes

This habitat is covered by the sea from time to time. Salty sea water may cover parts of a saltmarsh every day, or just occasionally. Wading birds and wildfowl, such as ducks and geese, feed and breed in saltmarshes.

Saltmarsh plants have to be able to cope with salty water.

Birds such as Canada geese visit river estuaries at low tide, looking for food.

Estuaries, mud and sand flats

Every time the tide goes out, the retreating water leaves behind deposits of mud or sand. These deposits build up to create areas of sediment called flats. Estuaries are formed where rivers flow into the sea and are rich in wildlife.

How to use this book

Seashore detectives like to keep records of what they have seen, and you can do that by filling in the pages of this book. There are spaces for your notes, sketches and photographs.

Photofile
Photos of the seashore wildlife in its natural habitat, plus extra information. Some provide examples of variant species you could spot.

Seen it?
Once you've spotted a species, record it by ticking the *Seen It* circle.

My observations
Make notes about your sightings and surroundings here. For example, write down which beach you have visited, the time of day and also the weather – this will help if you decide to search for the same animal or plant, as certain species prefer specific conditions. Then you can make a note of what you have found. Lastly, describe its appearance.

MY OBSERVATIONS

Location:

Time:

The weather is:

What have I found?

What does it look like?

SEEN IT?

The velvet swimming crab is a grazer and a predator. It hides in seaweed or anemones, looking for prey.

MY DRAWINGS AND PHOTOS

My drawings and photos
Fill these spaces with your sketches and photographs.

Photos: Concentrate on taking photos of the whole plant or animal and its habitat. You will need plenty of sunlight, but avoid very bright sunshine because it causes strong black shadows. Make sure your shadow is not cast over your find.

Drawings: Use a soft pencil, such as 2B, because the lead is easy to rub out. You don't need to draw the whole animal or plant, you could draw a close-up of an insect's head, for example, or a crab's claw.

66

Main text
Every right-hand page
has a main paragraph
to introduce each
species.

Colour coding
The entries in this book are
organised by type, either by
animal group or similar species.
The pages of each section are
colour-coded, making it easy to
identify your find.

Velvet swimming crab *Necora puber*

Most crabs scuttle along the shore and seabed, hiding beneath rocks or digging into sand. Velvet swimming crabs can also run extremely quickly and they are good swimmers. Their last pair of legs are flattened and covered with hairs, to help them swim. Velvet swimming crabs are best left alone – they can be aggressive if touched and their strong pincers can give a painful injury.

TYPE Decapod
SIZE Length and width up to 8 cm
HABITAT Low shore and shallow water, especially among rocks
FOUND Atlantic Ocean, English Channel, North Sea
OTHER NAMES Velvet crab, devil crab

Fact file
This box gives you key
information about each
seashore species.

hind legs are flattened

legs fringed with fine hairs

brown-red carapace

Illustrations
Detailed artwork shows the
key features of each species.

red eyes

WARNING SIGNS

Beware! Don't touch
You must not touch the species
that have this symbol. They may
have sharp spines, stinging
tentacles or large pincers.

BEWARE!
DON'T TOUCH

strong, slender pincers

I saw this crustacean in: Spring ○ Summer ○ Autumn ○ Winter ○

67

Which season?
Tick here to record the season
you've spotted each species in.

**Rare, Protected and
Specially Protected**
You must only observe the
wildlife that has this symbol
because they are endangered,
and you could be breaking the
law. Some birds have been
afforded the 'specially protected'
status by the UK Biodiversity
Action Plan to protect
vulnerable species.

MY OBSERVATIONS

Location: _____

Time: _____

The weather is: _____

_____

What have I found? _____

_____

What does it look like? _____

_____

_____

_____

MY DRAWINGS AND PHOTOS

The tips of the fronds of bladder wrack are often paler in colour, and covered with round, swollen areas. These are used in reproduction.

Bladder wrack _Fucus vesiculosus_

This seaweed is common on rocky shores and is easy to identify. When the tide goes out, slippery strands of bladder wrack stretch out over stones and pebbles. The fronds are covered in pairs of round air bladders, which help them to float. This allows the seaweed to reach the sunlight and grow, but the air bladders may be absent if exposed to large waves.

TYPE Brown algae

SIZE 50–200 cm

HABITAT Rocky shores especially on the middle-shore, estuaries

FOUND Atlantic Ocean, North Sea, English Channel

OTHER NAMES Rock wrack

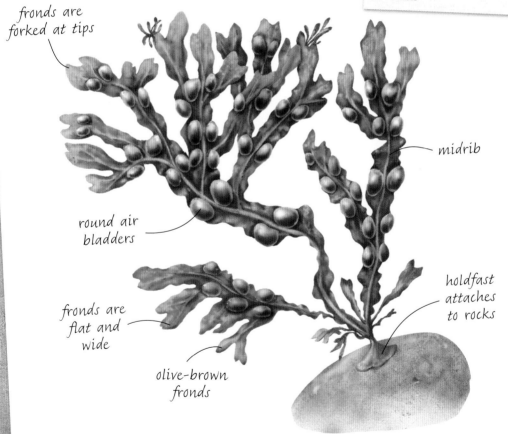

fronds are forked at tips

round air bladders

fronds are flat and wide

olive-brown fronds

midrib

holdfast attaches to rocks

I saw this seaweed in: Spring ○ Summer ○ Autumn ○ Winter ○

MY OBSERVATIONS

Location: _____

Time: _____

The weather is: _____

_____

What have I found? _____

_____

What does it look like? _____

_____

_____

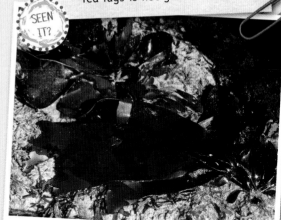

Red rags seaweed look similar to dulse. Whereas dulse is often eaten dried or fresh, and used in cooking, red rags is not good to eat.

SEEN IT?

MY DRAWINGS AND PHOTOS

Dulse *Palmaria palmata*

This commonly found seaweed can be used as food. Its long, leathery fronds can grow quite wide, and become tougher as they age. The ends of the fronds are divided into flat lobes and are usually paler than the rest of the alga. Dulse can be found on rocky shores at low tide and in shallow waters. Long, narrow lobes indicate that the seaweed has been exposed to strong waves.

TYPE Red algae

SIZE 20–50 cm

HABITAT Lower shore, especially rocky shores

FOUND Atlantic Ocean, English Channel, North Sea

OTHER NAMES Dilsk, red dulse

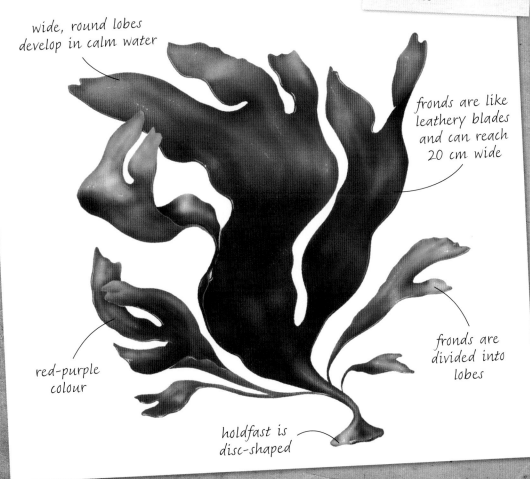

wide, round lobes develop in calm water

fronds are like leathery blades and can reach 20 cm wide

red-purple colour

fronds are divided into lobes

holdfast is disc-shaped

MY OBSERVATIONS

Location: _____

Time: _____

The weather is: _____

_____

What have I found? _____

_____

What does it look like? _____

_____

_____

Knotted wrack is often covered with tufts of red seaweed called *Polysiphonia*. As *Polysiphonia* grows, it damages the wrack.

SEEN IT?

MY DRAWINGS AND PHOTOS

Knotted wrack *Ascophyllum nodosum*

Often found on rocky shores, knotted wrack is recognisable by the two types of swelling along its slender fronds. The large oval swellings are gas bladders, and are full of air. This helps the fronds to float and reach sunlight. The smaller swellings are paler in colour and help the alga reproduce. Knotted wrack rarely grows on shores with big waves and strong winds.

TYPE Brown algae

SIZE 30–200 cm

HABITAT Middle and upper shore, in rocky places

FOUND Widespread around the British Isles

OTHER NAMES Egg wrack, knotted kelp

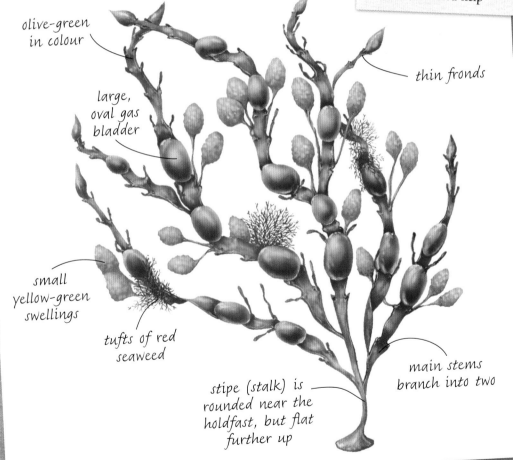

olive-green in colour

thin fronds

large, oval gas bladder

small yellow-green swellings

tufts of red seaweed

stipe (stalk) is rounded near the holdfast, but flat further up

main stems branch into two

I saw this seaweed in: Spring O   Summer O   Autumn O   Winter O

MY OBSERVATIONS

Location: _____

Time: _____

The weather is: _____

_____

What have I found? _____

_____

What does it look like? _____

_____

_____

Oarweeds belong to a family of seaweeds called kelps. Underwater forests of kelp make great places for sea creatures to shelter.

SEEN IT?

MY DRAWINGS AND PHOTOS

Oarweed *Laminaria digitata*

This tough seaweed survives well in coastal areas where there are strong waves and wind. Oarweed does not have roots, but is attached to the seabed or to rocks by a secure holdfast. It has thick, glossy fronds and a round stipe (stalk) that can bend without snapping. These algae provide a seashore habitat where small animals can live and shelter.

TYPE Brown algae

SIZE Up to 200 cm

HABITAT Rocks on the lower shore and water up to 6 m deep

FOUND Coastal waters all around British Isles

OTHER NAMES Tangle, tangleweed

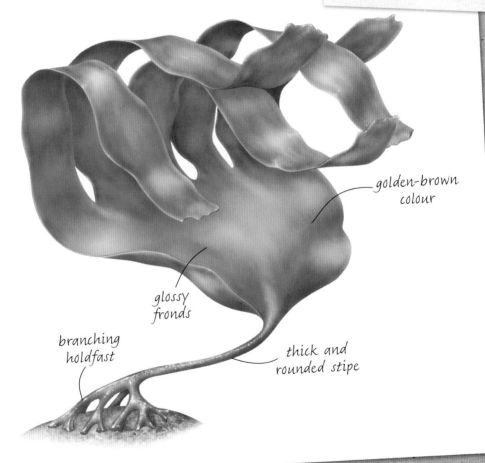

golden-brown colour

glossy fronds

branching holdfast

thick and rounded stipe

I saw this seaweed in: Spring O   Summer O   Autumn O   Winter O

MY OBSERVATIONS

Location: _____

Time: _____

The weather is: _____

_____

What have I found? _____

_____

What does it look like? _____

_____

_____

Each plant is either male or female – the margins of a male plant's fronds are light in colour, but a female has dark margins.

SEEN IT?

MY DRAWINGS AND PHOTOS

Sea lettuce *Ulva lactuca*

The appearance of its light green, delicate-looking fronds gives sea lettuce its common name. It grows attached to rocks and pebbles at the top of the shore. Sea lettuce can also survive at river mouths and in shallow salty waters inland. It is sometimes collected for use as a food, and is used in soups.

TYPE Green algae

SIZE 15–40 cm

HABITAT Rocky shores, estuaries, rock pools

FOUND Widespread around the British Isles

OTHER NAMES None

larger fronds grow in sheltered water

light can pass through very thin fronds

bright green colour

margins may be white or dark green

small holdfast

MY OBSERVATIONS

Location:

Time:

The weather is:

What have I found?

What does it look like?

In autumn many glasswort change colour. Some types turn red, others turn purple-pink, orange-red or yellowish.

SEEN IT?

MY DRAWINGS AND PHOTOS

Glasswort *Salicornia europaea*

Plants that live near the sea often have salty water around their roots. Only certain salt-loving plants, such as glasswort, can cope with these conditions, and they often have tiny leaves that grow close to thick, fleshy stems – this helps them store fresh water. Glasswort plants look like small cacti and can be found growing in estuaries.

TYPE Salt-loving family

HEIGHT Up to 30 cm

HABITAT Salty places including mud flats, estuaries and saltmarshes

FLOWERS August to September

FRUIT Tiny seeds with hooked hairs

OTHER NAMES Marsh samphire

tiny flowers

segments are plump and full of water

these small scales are tiny leaves

spikes grow upwards

in spring and summer the stems are bright green and plump

I saw this plant in: Spring O   Summer O   Autumn O   Winter O

MY OBSERVATIONS

Location: _____

Time: _____

The weather is: _____

_____

What have I found? _____

_____

What does it look like? _____

_____

_____

_____

SEEN IT?

Areas with marram grass not only support sand dunes – they provide shelter and homes for many insects, animals and plants.

MY DRAWINGS AND PHOTOS

Marram grass *Ammophila arenaria*

You can find marram grass growing on dunes all over the world. Its thick, green clumps of spiky shoots and leaves help build up dunes by binding the sand and preventing it from blowing away in the wind. These plants can survive in dry, sandy habitats because the leaves are coated in a wax-like substance that reduces water loss.

TYPE Grass family

HEIGHT Up to 120 cm

HABITAT Sand dunes

FLOWERS May to August

FRUIT Small seeds in a cluster at tip of a flower spike

OTHER NAMES Beach grass

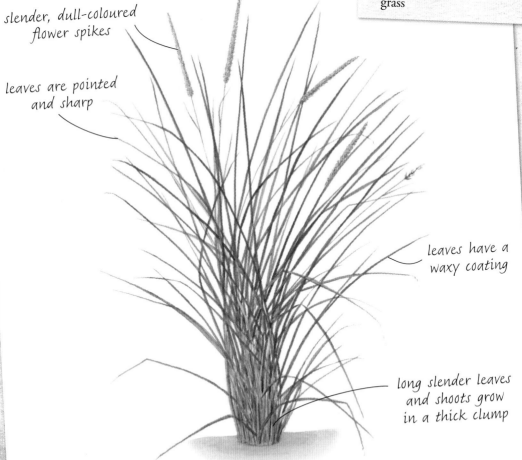

slender, dull-coloured flower spikes

leaves are pointed and sharp

leaves have a waxy coating

long slender leaves and shoots grow in a thick clump

I saw this plant in: Spring O Summer O Autumn O Winter O

MY OBSERVATIONS

Location: _____

Time: _____

The weather is: _____

_____

What have I found? _____

_____

What does it look like? _____

_____

_____

_____

Bog pimpernels are a similar species. They have small pink flowers and grow on boggy ground, dunes and moorland.

SEEN IT?

MY DRAWINGS AND PHOTOS

Scarlet pimpernel *Anagallis arvensis*

This delicate plant is common in gardens, farmland and parks, but it also grows on sand dunes and stony places in coastal areas. These pretty plants have small red flowers that only open when it is sunny. Scarlet pimpernels do not grow tall, but creep over the ground, covering it in green stems and leaves. Insects are attracted to the flowers in spring and summer.

TYPE Primrose family

HEIGHT Up to 20 cm

HABITAT Farms, grassland and sand dunes

FLOWERS Small, red flowers from May to September

FRUIT Tiny brown capsules

OTHER NAMES Red chickweed, red pimpernel, shepherd's clock, poor man's weatherglass

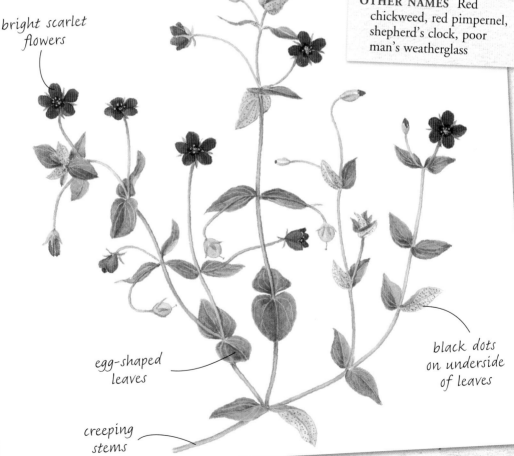

bright scarlet flowers

egg-shaped leaves

creeping stems

black dots on underside of leaves

MY OBSERVATIONS

Location: _____

Time: _____

The weather is: _____

_____

What have I found? _____

_____

What does it look like? _____

_____

_____

_____

After a sea kale has flowered, the seed pods slowly ripen. They dry out and up to 10,000 seeds are released.

SEEN IT?

MY DRAWINGS AND PHOTOS

Sea kale *Crambe maritima*

Often found on shingle beaches, sea kale can also survive in the dry, sandy parts of the upper shore. Its thick leaves are able to store water and have a waxy coating on their surface, which stops too much water evaporating. Sea kale rarely flowers before reaching five years of age. This plant used to be steamed and eaten, but it is now rare and should never be picked.

TYPE Cabbage family

HEIGHT Up to 100 cm

HABITAT Upper sandy or shingle shores, pebbly beaches, cliffs

FLOWERS White flowers from June to August

FRUIT Round, green fruits

OTHER NAMES Colewort, flowering sea kale

waxy coating on the leaves

large, thick leaves are green or purple

plant grows in a dome shape

clusters of white flowers

RARE & PROTECTED

I saw this plant in: Spring O Summer O Autumn O Winter O

MY OBSERVATIONS

Location: _____

Time: _____

The weather is: _____

_____

What have I found? _____

_____

What does it look like? _____

_____

_____

_____

Long-tongued bees are attracted to the pink flowers, and pollinate them. Pigeons and doves eat the pea-sized seeds.

SEEN IT?

MY DRAWINGS AND PHOTOS

Sea pea Lathyrus japonicus

Pretty sea pea plants provide colour to dry areas of shingle beaches. Their delicate leaves and tendrils spread out in clumps up to 2 metres wide. Sea peas rarely flower before their third summer. The pea-like seeds are carried by seawater to new areas, and can survive for up to five years before they start to grow into new plants.

TYPE Pea family

HEIGHT Up to 20 cm

HABITAT Upper shore, dry shingle, sandy banks

FLOWERS Pink/purple flowers from May to August

FRUIT Pods containing seeds

OTHER NAMES Beach pea

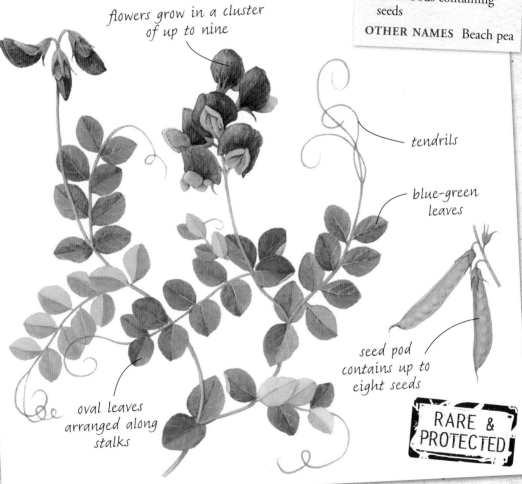

flowers grow in a cluster of up to nine

tendrils

blue-green leaves

seed pod contains up to eight seeds

oval leaves arranged along stalks

RARE & PROTECTED

I saw this plant in: Spring O   Summer O   Autumn O   Winter O

MY OBSERVATIONS

Location: _____

Time: _____

The weather is: _____

_____

What have I found? _____

_____

What does it look like? _____

_____

_____

_____

On cloudy days and at night, the leaves of a silverweed plant may be closed. On sunny days they open up.

SEEN IT?

MY DRAWINGS AND PHOTOS

Silverweed *Potentilla anserine*

This creeping plant grows in grassy areas and on bare ground, including sand and shingle shores. It grows best on damp ground but can survive periods of dry weather. The leaves are feathery and divided into many pairs of leaflets, which are covered in fine hairs. Long, creeping stems, called stolons, trail along the ground between the leaves and flowers.

TYPE Rose family
HEIGHT 5–20 cm
HABITAT Cliffs, upper shingle and sandy shores
FLOWERS May to August
FRUIT Dry and papery
OTHER NAMES Silverweed cinquefoil

up to 12 leaflets on a leaf

five yellow petals

silvery hairs on the leaves

long, creeping stems have a red tint

I saw this plant in: Spring ○ Summer ○ Autumn ○ Winter ○

MY OBSERVATIONS

Location: _____

Time: _____

The weather is: _____

_____

What have I found? _____

_____

What does it look like? _____

_____

_____

_____

MY DRAWINGS AND PHOTOS

Most thrift flowers are pink, but they may also be white or red. They thrive on cliffs and are also popular garden plants.

SEEN IT?

Thrift *Armeria maritima*

Thrift can survive on upper shores and cliffs because it likes dry habitats. It is easy to identify with its candyfloss pink flowerheads, which grow above a dense mat of leaves. The plant forms a round, cushion-like clump and the leaves remain once the flowers have died back. As the flowerheads age they become paler in colour, dry and papery.

TYPE Thrift family

HEIGHT Up to 20 cm

HABITAT Rocky places, cliffs

FLOWERS Round pink flowerheads from April to October

FRUIT Capsules

OTHER NAMES Sea thrift, sea pink, sea cushion

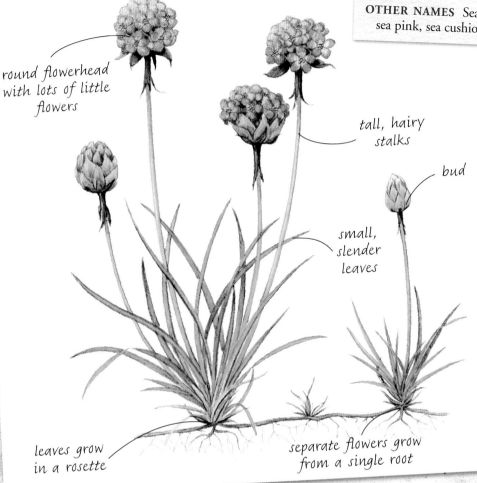

round flowerhead with lots of little flowers

tall, hairy stalks

bud

small, slender leaves

leaves grow in a rosette

separate flowers grow from a single root

I saw this plant in: Spring ○ Summer ○ Autumn ○ Winter ○

MY OBSERVATIONS

Location:

Time:

The weather is:

What have I found?

What does it look like?

The best place to find an anemone is in a rock pool, along with other animals such as periwinkles, limpets and small shanny fish.

SEEN IT?

MY DRAWINGS AND PHOTOS

Beadlet anemone _Actinia equina_

Anemones are related to coral polyps, the tiny animals that build coral reefs. They have soft bodies, but protect themselves with stinging tentacles, which they also use to kill and catch prey. When anemones are underwater their tentacles are obvious, but they quickly withdraw if disturbed or when the tide goes out. Their stings can be painful – keep a look out for them when exploring rock pools.

TYPE Cnidarian

HEIGHT Up to 7 cm

HABITAT Rock pools, rocky shores, to depths of 20 m

FOUND Widespread on British rocky shores

OTHER NAMES Red sea anemone

open with tentacles extended

tentacles in rows around mouth

closed with tentacles withdrawn

body is called the column

ring of blue dots at top of column

attached to rock by strong sucker on base

colour may be red, brown, orange or green

BEWARE! DON'T TOUCH!

I saw this anemone in: Spring ○ Summer ○ Autumn ○ Winter ○

MY OBSERVATIONS

Location: _____

Time: _____

The weather is: _____

_____

What have I found? _____

_____

What does it look like? _____

_____

_____

_____

Offshore, up to 2000 brittlestars can live in one square metre. These strange-looking creatures can be found washed ashore after storms.

SEEN IT?

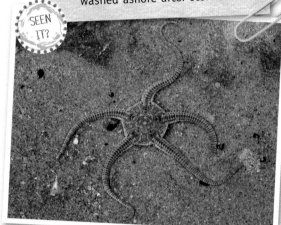

MY DRAWINGS AND PHOTOS

Brittlestar _Ophiothrix fragilis_

These unusual animals often live in large groups and gather under rocks and in seaweed. If you look under large stones or in crooks and crevices at the very lowest tide, you may be able to find a brittlestar hiding from its predators. Brittlestars are very delicate and should not be touched as they are covered in spines and easily damaged.

TYPE Echinoderm

SIZE 15–22 cm wide

HABITAT Lower shore and to depths of 150 m

FOUND Around British coastline except some eastern and southern areas

OTHER NAMES Common brittlestar

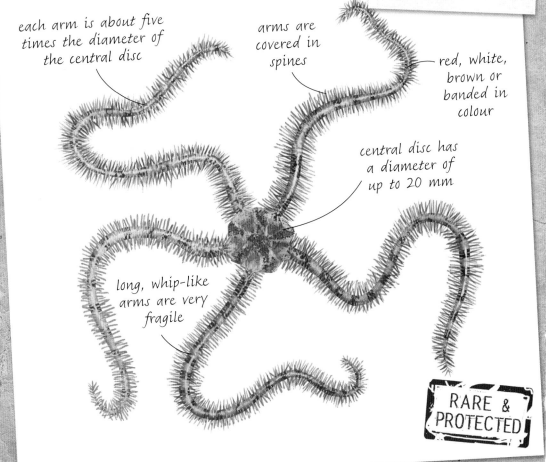

each arm is about five times the diameter of the central disc

arms are covered in spines

red, white, brown or banded in colour

central disc has a diameter of up to 20 mm

long, whip-like arms are very fragile

RARE & PROTECTED

MY OBSERVATIONS

Location: _____

Time: _____

The weather is: _____

_____

What have I found? _____

_____

What does it look like? _____

_____

_____

_____

SEEN IT?

Shore urchins are a relative of the edible sea urchin. These spiky creatures have green spines with violet tips and are found on rocky shores.

MY DRAWINGS AND PHOTOS

Edible sea urchin *Echinus esculentus*

Covered in sharp spines, urchins can cause painful injuries. The shell-like tests of dead urchins are sometimes washed up on shore. Urchins feed on seaweed and small animals. They move along the seafloor and graze as they move, grinding up food with their powerful mouthparts.

TYPE Echinoderm

SIZE Up to 10 cm wide

HABITAT Lower shore, rock pools, and to depths of 50 m

FOUND Widespread around British coast

OTHER NAMES None

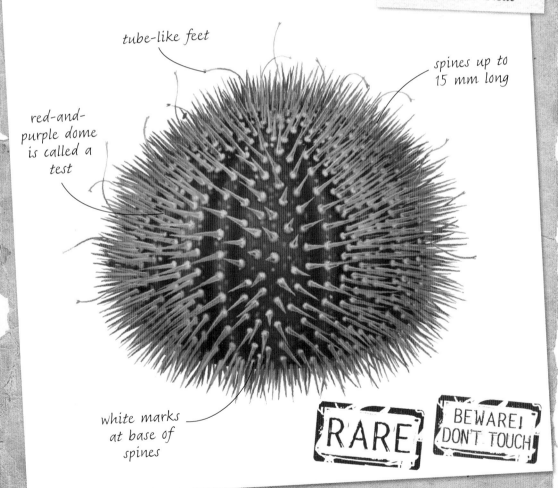

tube-like feet

spines up to 15 mm long

red-and-purple dome is called a test

white marks at base of spines

RARE

BEWARE! DON'T TOUCH

MY OBSERVATIONS

Location:

Time:

The weather is:

What have I found?

What does it look like?

SEEN IT?

Sometimes, big tides wash starfish onto a beach. Once stranded, they are unlikely to make it back to the water, and they die.

MY DRAWINGS AND PHOTOS

Starfish *Asterias rubens*

These widespread creatures can be found on sand, gravel and rocky coasts at low tide, as well as in rock pools. They are commonly found near mussels and barnacles. Starfish use their sense of smell to find prey, and eat molluscs by ripping open their shells using the suckers on the undersides of their arms. They can live up to ten years, and often gather in large groups.

TYPE Echinoderm

SIZE 10–50 cm wide

HABITAT Lower shore to depths of 200 m

FOUND Widespread around British coast

OTHER NAMES Common starfish

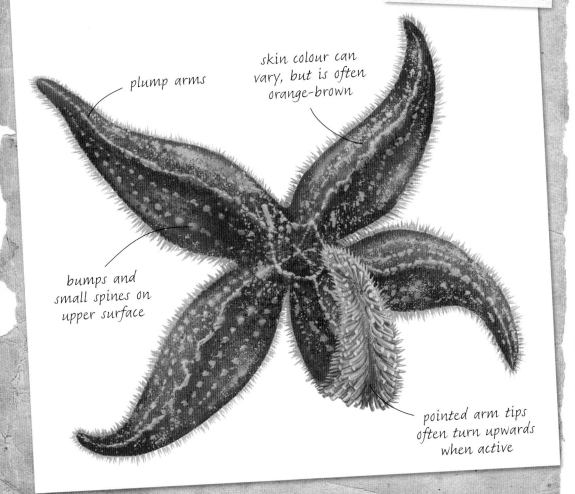

plump arms

skin colour can vary, but is often orange-brown

bumps and small spines on upper surface

pointed arm tips often turn upwards when active

I saw this starfish in: Spring ○ Summer ○ Autumn ○ Winter ○

MY OBSERVATIONS

Location: _____

Time: _____

The weather is: _____

_____

What have I found? _____

_____

What does it look like?

_____

_____

_____

_____

Empty cockle shells are often washed up onto beaches. They can be found in different sizes depending on their age.

SEEN IT?

MY DRAWINGS AND PHOTOS

Common cockle *Cerastoderma edule*

It is unusual to find a live cockle on the shore, but their shells are easy to spot. The living animal inhabits two shells that are tightly joined together when exposed to the air, such as at low tide. Underwater, the shells open so the animal can take tiny particles of food from the water. Most cockles live for about three years. They are preyed upon by seabirds such as oystercatchers.

TYPE Bivalve

SIZE Up to 5 cm long

HABITAT Lower shore in muddy or sandy places, estuaries

FOUND Atlantic Ocean, English Channel, North Sea

OTHER NAMES Edible cockle

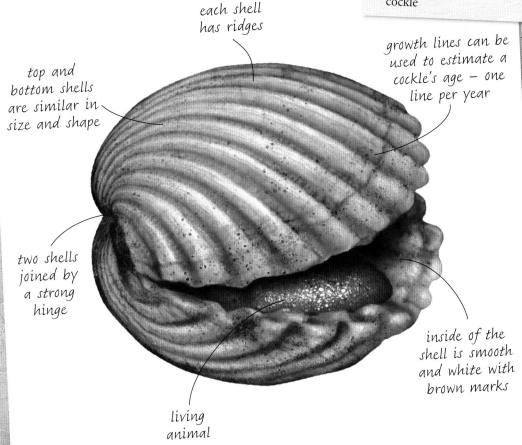

each shell has ridges

growth lines can be used to estimate a cockle's age – one line per year

top and bottom shells are similar in size and shape

two shells joined by a strong hinge

inside of the shell is smooth and white with brown marks

living animal

I saw this mollusc in: Spring ○   Summer ○   Autumn ○   Winter ○

MY OBSERVATIONS

Location: _____

Time: _____

The weather is: _____

_____

What have I found? _____

_____

What does it look like? _____

_____

_____

_____

Limpets are grazers and move along rocks to feed on algae. As they graze, they may leave paths in the sand.

SEEN IT?

MY DRAWINGS AND PHOTOS

Common limpet *Patella vulgata*

Limpets belong to the same family as garden slugs and snails. They are found on rocky shores, where they stick firmly to rocks and can leave marks where they have rubbed the surface away. Limpets are protected by their cone-shaped shells and can withstand large waves. Those that live on the upper shore usually have taller shells than those that live on the lower shore.

TYPE Gastropod

SIZE Shell 5–7 cm long

HABITAT Rocks on middle and upper shore, estuaries

FOUND Widespread, especially on western coasts

OTHER NAMES None

shell is cone-shaped

grey, white or yellowish in colour

ridges come from the central point

growth lines

limpets move around using their foot

I saw this mollusc in: Spring ○ Summer ○ Autumn ○ Winter ○

MY OBSERVATIONS

Location: _____

Time: _____

The weather is: _____

_____

What have I found? _____

_____

What does it look like? _____

_____

_____

_____

At low tide, mussel beds are exposed to the air. When the tide comes in, the mussels will open their shells again to feed.

SEEN IT?

MY DRAWINGS AND PHOTOS

Common mussel *Mytilus edulis*

Like cockles, mussels are bivalves — the animal lives inside two shells that are joined together. They attach themselves to rocky surfaces and open their shells when underwater to feed. Mussels are often found living together in large numbers — these places are called mussel beds. They are preyed upon by seabirds, dog whelks, starfish and sea urchins. Humans also eat mussels.

TYPE Bivalve

SIZE Shell is up to 10 cm long

HABITAT Rocky shores and beds, estuaries

FOUND Widespread around British coasts

OTHER NAMES Blue mussel, edible mussel

blue-black in colour

triangular-shaped shell

bump in the shell near the hinge

hinge where top and bottom shells connect

inside is pearly and smooth

soft, fleshy body

I saw this mollusc in: Spring ○ Summer ○ Autumn ○ Winter ○

MY OBSERVATIONS

Location:

Time:

The weather is:

What have I found?

What does it look like?

Periwinkles often live together in large groups. They move along rocks, scraping seaweed off and feeding on it.

SEEN IT?

MY DRAWINGS AND PHOTOS

Common periwinkle *Littorina littorea*

These molluscs live on rocky shores and can withstand large waves. They can survive out of water for long periods because they have a flap that covers the opening to their shells. Young periwinkles are dark brown, but become paler in colour with age. These molluscs feed on small particles of food in the sea and seaweed, especially sea lettuce.

TYPE Gastropod

SIZE Height of shell 2–3 cm

HABITAT Rocky shores, stones, in seaweed, estuaries

FOUND Widespread around British coasts

OTHER NAMES Edible periwinkle

shell develops a smoother surface with age

snail-like body

spire

dark lines around the spire

white around lip

neat, small shell with a single opening

MY OBSERVATIONS

Location: _____

Time: _____

The weather is: _____

_____

What have I found? _____

_____

What does it look like? _____

_____

_____

_____

Dog whelks lay groups of eggs on rocks during spring. These molluscs can live for up to seven years.

SEEN IT?

MY DRAWINGS AND PHOTOS

Dog whelk *Nucella lapillus*

These small predators are related to garden snails, but unlike their cousins they do not feed on grass. Dog whelks hunt small animals, such as barnacles and mussels. They are even able to bore through the shell of another animal to reach the soft flesh inside. Whelk shells are often washed up on the shore.

TYPE Gastropod

SIZE Shell up to 3 cm long

HABITAT Rocky shores, especially middle shore

FOUND Widespread around British coasts

OTHER NAMES Atlantic dog winkle

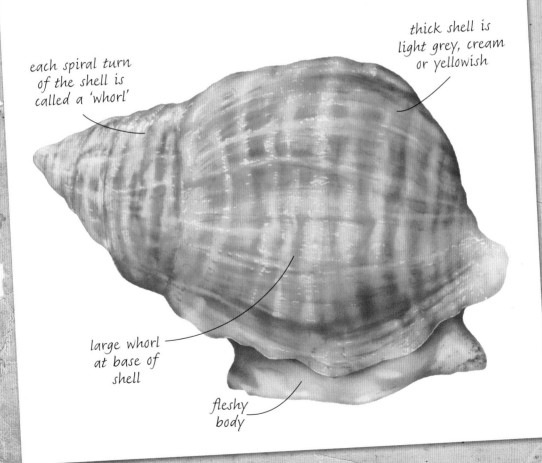

each spiral turn of the shell is called a 'whorl'

thick shell is light grey, cream or yellowish

large whorl at base of shell

fleshy body

I saw this mollusc in: Spring ○   Summer ○   Autumn ○   Winter ○

MY OBSERVATIONS

Location: _____

Time: _____

The weather is: _____
_____

What have I found? _____
_____

What does it look like? _____
_____
_____
_____

Painted topshells look bright and shiny because the animal uses its foot to wipe over the shell surface and clean it.

SEEN IT?

MY DRAWINGS AND PHOTOS

Painted topshell *Calliostoma zizyphinum*

Topshells usually have coloured or patterned shells. They often have streaks or blotches of colour, and some shells are mostly white. The inside of the shell is pearly and smooth and the opening is protected by a flap, so the animal can survive when the tide goes out. Painted topshells are most commonly found amongst the holdfasts of seaweeds, where they graze.

TYPE Gastropod

SIZE Height of shell is up to 3 cm

HABITAT Rocky shores, especially low shore and among seaweed

FOUND Widespread around British coasts

OTHER NAMES None

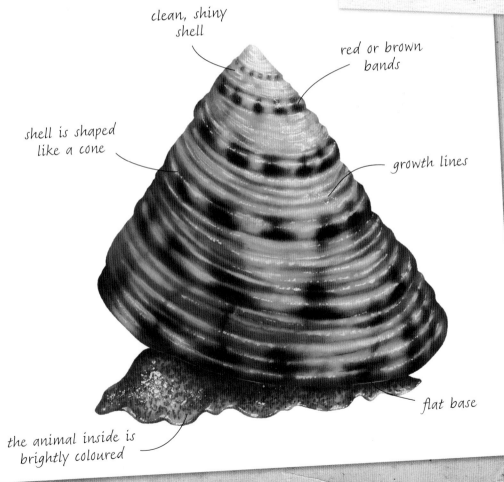

clean, shiny shell

red or brown bands

shell is shaped like a cone

growth lines

the animal inside is brightly coloured

flat base

I saw this mollusc in: Spring ○ Summer ○ Autumn ○ Winter ○

MY OBSERVATIONS

Location: _____

Time: _____

The weather is: _____

_____

What have I found? _____

_____

What does it look like? _____

_____

_____

_____

Plants and animals may live on a hermit crab's shell. Barnacles and sea anemones are common hitchhikers.

SEEN IT?

MY DRAWINGS AND PHOTOS

Hermit crab *Pagurus bernhardus*

These common coastal creatures are more closely related to lobsters than crabs. Their skins are quite soft, so they get extra protection by setting up home in empty shells. Their bodies are twisted to fit comfortably inside. Occasionally, they find a bigger, better shell and do a quick swap. These crustaceans forage on the seashore looking for carrion (dead animals) to eat.

TYPE Decapod

SIZE 2–6 cm long

HABITAT Shallow water, rock pools, rocky shores, sandy shores

FOUND Atlantic Ocean, North Sea, English Channel

OTHER NAMES Common hermit crab, soldier crab

sensitive antennae

empty mollusc shell used to protect soft body

body inside the shell is covered by a soft outer skin, or carapace

red to brown in colour

walking legs

right pincer larger than the left

first two legs are used as pincers

I saw this crustacean in: Spring ○ Summer ○ Autumn ○ Winter ○

MY OBSERVATIONS

Location: _____

Time: _____

The weather is: _____

_____

What have I found? _____

_____

What does it look like? _____

_____

_____

_____

The empty shells of dead barnacles have lost their terminal plates. Living barnacles survive alongside the dead ones.

SEEN IT?

MY DRAWINGS AND PHOTOS

Northern acorn barnacle

Semibalanus balanoides

*I*t is unusual to see a live barnacle, but it is easy to find their tough, protective shells. Barnacles cover many seashore rocks and can even be found growing on mollusc shells. When the tide is out, the barnacle shell is closed, but once underwater it opens and the tiny animal pokes its feathery limbs out to feed on food particles floating in the seawater.

TYPE Cirriped

SIZE Up to 15 mm wide

HABITAT Middle to upper shore, in rocky places

FOUND Atlantic Ocean, especially in northern areas

OTHER NAMES None

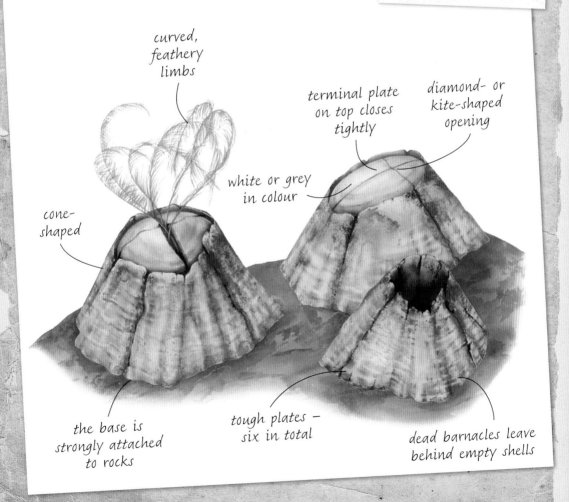

curved, feathery limbs

terminal plate on top closes tightly

diamond- or kite-shaped opening

white or grey in colour

cone-shaped

the base is strongly attached to rocks

tough plates – six in total

dead barnacles leave behind empty shells

I saw this crustacean in: Spring O   Summer O   Autumn O   Winter O

MY OBSERVATIONS

Location: _____

Time: _____

The weather is: _____

_____

What have I found? _____

_____

What does it look like? _____

_____

_____

_____

Large sand hoppers – *Talitrus saltator* – bury themselves in sand, and can dig down to depths of 30 cm.

SEEN IT?

MY DRAWINGS AND PHOTOS

Sand hopper *Orchestia gammarellus*

Also known as beach fleas, these small creatures often gather in large numbers along the strandline on a beach. This marks the highest place that the tide reaches. Seaweed, shells and stones collect here. During the day, sand hoppers mostly stay hidden, buried in the sand – but in the evening they emerge to look for food, hopping around between the seaweed.

TYPE Amphipod

SIZE Up to 18 mm long

HABITAT On all shores, especially where seaweed is stranded

FOUND All coastal regions

OTHER NAMES Beach hopper, sand flea, beach flea

two pairs of antennae – one much longer than the other

large, black eyes

body is divided into segments

large pincers on the third pair of legs

seven pairs of jointed legs

short tail

I saw this crustacean in: Spring ○　Summer ○　Autumn ○　Winter ○

MY OBSERVATIONS

Location: _____

Time: _____

The weather is: _____

_____

What have I found? _____

_____

What does it look like? _____

_____

_____

_____

Edible crabs are larger than shore crabs and grow up to 25 cm wide. Their claws and undersides are orange-red.

SEEN IT?

MY DRAWINGS AND PHOTOS

Shore crab *Carcinus maenas*

Crabs have five pairs of legs, although the front pair has powerful pincers. They use their pincers to fight and catch prey. Shore crabs feed on molluscs, worms or other crustaceans. They also eat the remains of dead fish that have been washed ashore. During summer, you are likely to find young crabs as well as older adults on the shore and in rock pools.

TYPE Decapod

SIZE Up to 10 cm wide

HABITAT All shores and shallow water, estuaries

FOUND Atlantic Ocean, English Channel, North Sea

OTHER NAMES Addlers, applejacks, European green crab

pointed hind legs are used to grip onto pebbles

can be green or brown

tough outer skin (carapace) is wider than it is long

second and third pairs of legs are long

eyes on stalks can move around

powerful pincers on first pair of legs

MY OBSERVATIONS

Location: _____

Time: _____

The weather is: _____

_____

What have I found? _____

_____

What does it look like? _____

_____

_____

_____

Shrimps walk along the seabed looking for small worms, molluscs and crustaceans to feed on.

SEEN IT?

MY DRAWINGS AND PHOTOS

Shrimp _Crangon crangon_

Shrimps can be hard to spot, because they are almost transparent (see-through) and very well camouflaged. These small crustaceans spend most of the day hiding in the sand, emerging at sunset to feed. Shrimps are food for many seabirds that wade through shallow water, probing the sand and mud with their bills.

TYPE Decapod

SIZE 3–5 cm long

HABITAT Shallow water, rock pools

FOUND Atlantic Ocean, North Sea, Irish Sea

OTHER NAMES Grey shrimp, brown shrimp

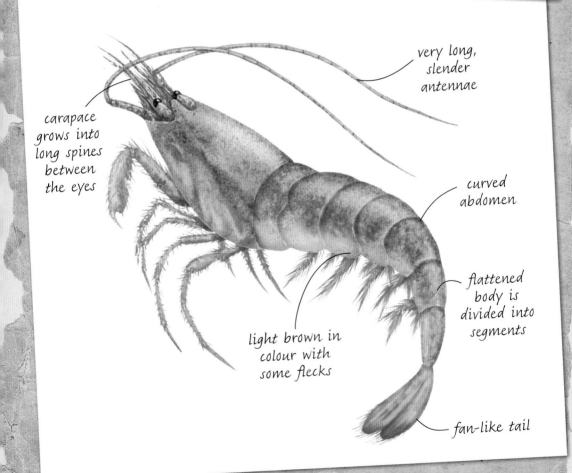

very long, slender antennae

carapace grows into long spines between the eyes

curved abdomen

flattened body is divided into segments

light brown in colour with some flecks

fan-like tail

I saw this crustacean in: Spring ○ Summer ○ Autumn ○ Winter ○

MY OBSERVATIONS

Location: _____

Time: _____

The weather is: _____

_____

What have I found? _____

_____

What does it look like? _____

_____

_____

_____

The velvet swimming crab is a grazer and a predator. It hides in seaweed or anemones, looking for prey.

SEEN IT?

MY DRAWINGS AND PHOTOS

Velvet swimming crab *Necora puber*

Most crabs scuttle along the shore and seabed, hiding beneath rocks or digging into sand. Velvet swimming crabs can also run extremely quickly and they are good swimmers. Their last pair of legs are flattened and covered with hairs, to help them swim. Velvet swimming crabs are best left alone – they can be aggressive if touched and their strong pincers can give a painful injury.

TYPE Decapod

SIZE Length and width up to 8 cm

HABITAT Low shore and shallow water, especially among rocks

FOUND Atlantic Ocean, English Channel, North Sea

OTHER NAMES Velvet crab, devil crab

hind legs are flattened

legs fringed with fine hairs

brown-red carapace

red eyes

strong, slender pincers

BEWARE! DON'T TOUCH

I saw this crustacean in: Spring O Summer O Autumn O Winter O

MY OBSERVATIONS

Location: _____

Time: _____

The weather is: _____

_____

What have I found? _____

_____

What does it look like? _____

_____

_____

_____

Common blues are most active in the sunshine, especially males. They fly around looking for flowers and females.

SEEN IT?

MY DRAWINGS AND PHOTOS

Common blue butterfly *Polyommatus icarus*

These pretty blue butterflies are most likely to be seen between May and September. They feed on nectar from large, flat-headed flowers and can be seen in coastal areas, especially around sand dunes. The larvae are green with yellow stripes along their sides and a dark line down their backs. They produce a substance from their skin that attracts ants, and in turn, the ants protect the larvae from predators.

TYPE Lepidopteran

WINGSPAN 3–4 cm long

HABITAT Sand dunes, sandy shores, cliffs, inland grasslands and gardens

FOUND Widespread in the UK

OTHER NAMES None

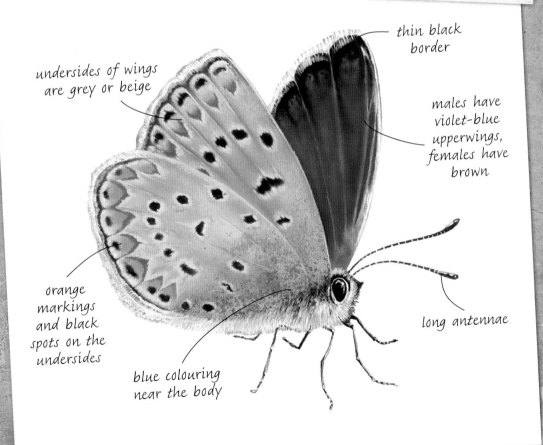

thin black border

undersides of wings are grey or beige

males have violet-blue upperwings, females have brown

orange markings and black spots on the undersides

blue colouring near the body

long antennae

I saw this insect in: Spring ○ Summer ○ Autumn ○ Winter ○

MY OBSERVATIONS

Location: _____

Time: _____

The weather is: _____

_____

What have I found?

_____

What does it look like?

_____

_____

_____

Once they land, grayling butterflies can be hard to spot as they blend into their surroundings.

SEEN IT?

MY DRAWINGS AND PHOTOS

Grayling butterfly *Hipparchia semele*

The grayling is quite a large butterfly, so it is easy to spot when in flight. Once it settles on sand, mud or rocks however, it becomes almost invisible. These insects prefer sunny, dry spots and the adults are active from June to the middle of September. Grayling caterpillars feed on grasses and are brown and cream in colour.

TYPE Lepidopteran

WINGSPAN Up to 6 cm

HABITAT Dunes, coastal paths, cliffs and hedges

FOUND Coasts, especially England and Wales and some inland areas such as heaths

OTHER NAMES None

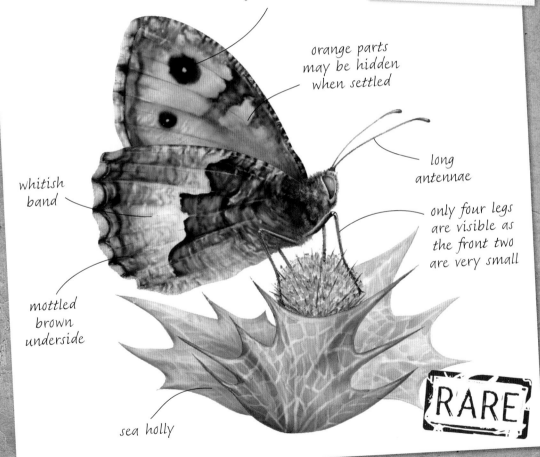

dark eye spots on forewings

orange parts may be hidden when settled

long antennae

only four legs are visible as the front two are very small

whitish band

mottled brown underside

sea holly

RARE

I saw this insect in: Spring ○ Summer ○ Autumn ○ Winter ○

MY OBSERVATIONS

Location: _____

Time: _____

The weather is: _____

_____

What have I found? _____

_____

What does it look like? _____

_____

_____

_____

When a green tiger beetle is disturbed it launches into short, buzzing flights. These beetles fly unusually fast.

SEEN IT?

MY DRAWINGS AND PHOTOS

Green tiger beetle *Cicindela campestris*

These brightly coloured beetles are common in the British Isles. They have a beautiful green metallic sheen and are easy to spot, especially on sunny summer days. Green tiger beetles have long legs and can run very fast when they chase other insects to eat. Green tiger beetles can also fly, and make a loud buzzing sound when in the air.

TYPE Coleopteran

SIZE Up to 15 mm long

HABITAT Sand dunes, sandy shores, cliffs

FOUND Coastal areas, inland grasslands and heathland throughout Britain

OTHER NAMES Common green tiger beetle

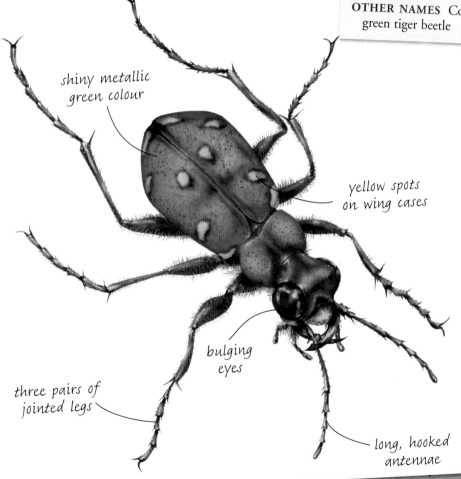

shiny metallic green colour

yellow spots on wing cases

bulging eyes

three pairs of jointed legs

long, hooked antennae

I saw this insect in: Spring ○ Summer ○ Autumn ○ Winter ○

MY OBSERVATIONS

Location: _____

Time: _____

The weather is: _____

_____

What have I found?

_____

What does it look like?

_____

_____

_____

The wasp uses its jaws to hold a caterpillar while stinging it. The small stinger is on the tip of the abdomen.

SEEN IT?

MY DRAWINGS AND PHOTOS

Red-banded sand wasp *Ammophila sabulosa*

With long black bodies and red bands, these stinging wasps are easy to identify. Red-banded sand wasps belong to the same family as bees and wasps. They use their stings to stun caterpillars, which are then dragged to the wasps' nests. The wasps then lay their eggs inside the caterpillars' bodies. When the eggs hatch the larvae feed on the live caterpillars.

TYPE Hymenopteran

SIZE Up to 25 mm long

HABITAT Sand dunes, sandy upper shores

FOUND Coasts and inland grasslands around Britain

OTHER NAMES Sand digger wasp

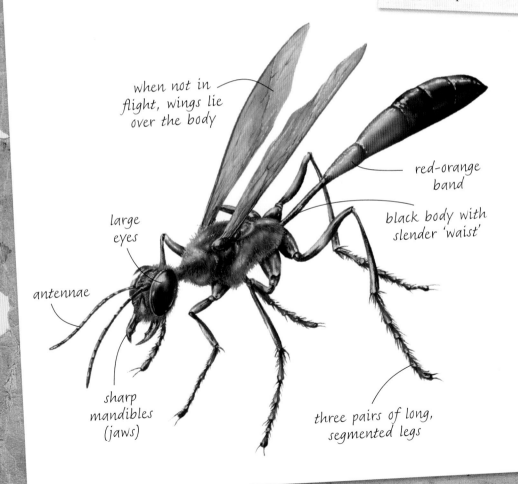

when not in flight, wings lie over the body

red-orange band

large eyes

black body with slender 'waist'

antennae

sharp mandibles (jaws)

three pairs of long, segmented legs

I saw this insect in: Spring ○ Summer ○ Autumn ○ Winter ○

MY OBSERVATIONS

Location: _____

Time: _____

The weather is: _____

_____

How many can I see? _____

_____

What is it/are they doing? _____

_____

_____

_____

Avocets build their nests in dry areas, but bring their chicks to muddy flats to feed.

MY DRAWINGS AND PHOTOS

Avocet *Recurvirostra avosetta*

These beautiful and elegant wading birds are found in coastal habitats, especially in eastern England. They have distinctive black-and-white plumage, long legs and unusually long bills, which they use to sweep through mud, searching for insects, shelled animals and worms to eat. Avocets became extinct in Britain in the 19th century, but they were successfully reintroduced to England in the 1940s.

SIZE 40–43 cm

WINGSPAN 67–77 cm

CALL Loud 'kloot' call

HABITAT Estuaries, coastal lagoons

BREEDING 3–4 eggs laid April to June

black cap and hind neck

white patches on wings

black bars on wings

long, black bill curves upwards

long, grey legs

RARE

I saw this bird in: Spring ○ Summer ○ Autumn ○ Winter ○

MY OBSERVATIONS

Location: _____

Time: _____

The weather is: _____

_____

How many can I see? _____

_____

What is it/are they doing? _____

_____

_____

_____

Both parents look after their eggs, but common tern chicks are mostly cared for, and fed, by their fathers.

SEEN IT?

MY DRAWINGS AND PHOTOS

Common tern *Sterna hirundo*

Sometimes called sea swallows because of the graceful way they fly, common terns swoop into the sea to catch fish. Elegant but aggressive, this bird is seen across Britain in the summer. It nests in noisy colonies and flies, often out at sea, in search of food. When they spot fish below them, terns plunge-dive into the water in pursuit of their prey.

SIZE 32–33 cm

WINGSPAN 82–95 cm

CALL 'Kreee-yar' or 'kik kik keer'

HABITAT Shingle beaches, estuaries, cliffs, inland gravel pits and reservoirs

BREEDING Up to 4 eggs laid around May

pale underwing with dark band at back edge

grey back to upperwing

black cap

bright red bill with a black tip

long, forked tail

orange feet

I saw this bird in: Spring ○ Summer ○ Autumn ○ Winter ○

MY OBSERVATIONS

Location: _____

Time: _____

The weather is: _____

_____

How many can I see? _____

_____

What is it/are they doing?

_____

_____

_____

It takes a great deal of muscle power and energy for a cormorant to lift its body out of the sea.

SEEN IT?

MY DRAWINGS AND PHOTOS

Cormorant *Phalacrocorax carbo*

These unusual-looking water birds have angular bodies and dark feathers. They are superb swimmers and live all around Britain's coasts. When a cormorant catches a fish, it shakes it before swallowing it whole. Cormorants have large, webbed feet used for swimming and for incubating their eggs, which they hold between the tops of their feet and their warm bodies.

SIZE 90 cm

WINGSPAN 130–160 cm

CALL Growling and crackling

HABITAT Rocky shores, estuaries, coastal lagoons and some inland lakes and reservoirs

BREEDING 3–4 eggs laid in April

glossy back

white cheeks and chin

long, yellow bill with small hook at tip

white patch in summer

long, broad tail

I saw this bird in: Spring ○ Summer ○ Autumn ○ Winter ○

MY OBSERVATIONS

Location: _____

Time: _____

The weather is: _____

_____

How many can I see? _____

_____

What is it/are they doing? _____

_____

_____

_____

Curlews are the largest of all wading birds in Europe. They are common around estuaries and coasts in January and February.

SEEN IT?

MY DRAWINGS AND PHOTOS

Curlew *Numenius arquata*

Some curlews live in Britain all year, in coastal areas and other water habitats. Others spend the winter here, and fly north when spring arrives. These waders are known for their beautiful spring song, which has been described as eerie or ghost-like. Curlews often gather in large numbers to feed, particularly at mud flats on estuaries.

SIZE 50–60 cm

WINGSPAN 80–100 cm

CALL Long slow 'cur-loo' or louder 'whoy'

HABITAT Estuaries, inland grasslands and uplands

BREEDING 4 eggs laid in spring

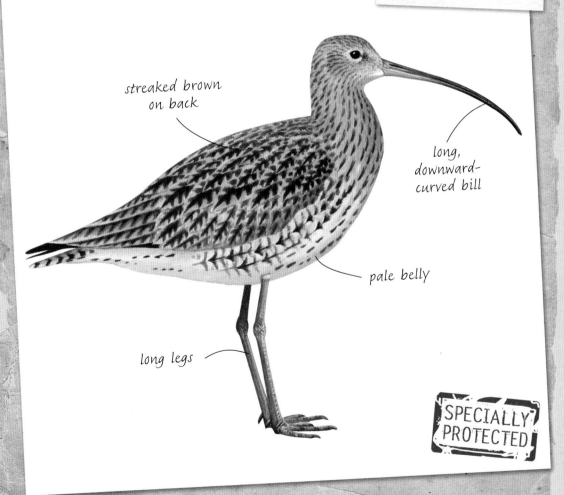

streaked brown on back

long, downward-curved bill

pale belly

long legs

SPECIALLY PROTECTED

I saw this bird in: Spring ○ Summer ○ Autumn ○ Winter ○

MY OBSERVATIONS

Location: _____

Time: _____

The weather is: _____

_____

How many can I see?

_____

What is it/are they doing?

_____

_____

_____

Herring gulls have bright yellow bills and an obvious red spot on the lower bill. They fly by soaring and gliding on the wind.

SEEN IT?

MY DRAWINGS AND PHOTOS

Herring gull *Larus argentatus*

These large birds are well known to holiday makers at seaside towns and beaches. Herring gulls have little fear of humans and will approach them for food. They have other ways of feeding though, such as trampling on mud to make worms come to the surface. In recent years, the number of herring gulls in Britain has dramatically fallen, although scientists are not sure why these birds are struggling to survive in coastal areas.

SIZE 55–67 cm

WINGSPAN 130–160 cm

CALL Loud 'kyow', 'ga-ga-ga'

HABITAT Cliffs, islands, mudflats, beaches especially in northern and eastern areas

BREEDING 2–3 eggs laid in May

pure-white head

yellow eyes

pale grey back

yellow bill with a red spot

black wing tips with white spots

pale pink legs

SPECIALLY PROTECTED

I saw this bird in: Spring ○ Summer ○ Autumn ○ Winter ○

MY OBSERVATIONS

Location:

Time:

The weather is:

How many can I see?

What is it/are they doing?

The knot (left) can look similar to a dunlin (right). Dunlins have longer bills and darker markings.

SEEN IT?

MY DRAWINGS AND PHOTOS

Knot *Calidris canutus*

Large flocks of knots gather around river mouths and estuaries during the winter months, especially in eastern areas. They spend spring and summer in the Arctic, where they breed, and at this time their plumage becomes much darker. Knots feed on small animals such as molluscs, crustaceans and worms, which they find in the muddy shores and mudflats at the coast.

SIZE 25 cm

WINGSPAN 47–54 cm

CALL 'Nutt' and 'twit-twit'

HABITAT Estuaries, muddy beaches

BREEDING 3–4 eggs laid May to July

pale stripe above eye

straight, long bill

feathers are mottled grey, white and light brown

stocky body

belly is paler than the back

short legs

I saw this bird in: Spring ⟳ Summer ⟳ Autumn ⟳ Winter ⟳

MY OBSERVATIONS

Location: _____

Time: _____

The weather is: _____

_____

How many can I see? _____

_____

What is it/are they doing? _____

_____

_____

_____

Limpets may be able to stick tightly to rock, but oystercatchers can use their strong bills to prise them off.

SEEN IT?

MY DRAWINGS AND PHOTOS

Oystercatcher *Haematopus ostralegus*

Bright, bold and noisy, oystercatchers are easy to identify. These sturdy birds live in coastal regions throughout the year and often form enormous flocks. They walk along seashores or mudflats with their heads down, searching for food. Oystercatchers use their strong bills to break open shellfish such as cockles and mussels. Despite their name, they do not appear to eat oysters.

SIZE 40–45 cm

WINGSPAN 80–85 cm

CALL Loud 'kleep kleep'

HABITAT Sandy, muddy and rocky beaches

BREEDING 2–3 eggs from April to July

red eye

long, bright orange bill

black-and-white plumage

large, bulky body

short, pale pink legs

I saw this bird in: Spring ○ Summer ○ Autumn ○ Winter ○

MY OBSERVATIONS

Location:

Time:

The weather is:

How many can I see?

What is it/are they doing?

Many redshanks in southwest England are winter visitors, flying in from Iceland.

SEEN IT?

MY DRAWINGS AND PHOTOS

Redshank *Tringa totanus*

These wading birds breed throughout the British Isles, especially in areas near water. When the breeding season is over, redshanks move towards the coast and estuaries. They wade through shallow water to search for molluscs, worms, crustaceans and insects to eat. Redshanks gather in large flocks, often perching on posts or breakwaters, and make loud alarm calls when disturbed.

SIZE 25–30 cm

WINGSPAN 45–50 cm

CALL 'Tu-yu-yu'

HABITAT Marshes, coastal mudflats, estuaries, uplands

BREEDING Lays a single brood of 4 eggs from April to July

grey-brown top feathers

white underparts

long red legs

long, straight bill is red at base and black at tip

I saw this bird in: Spring O Summer O Autumn O Winter O

MY OBSERVATIONS

Location:

Time:

The weather is:

How many can I see?

What is it/are they doing?

Found all year round, these plump little birds eat insects, crustaceans and worms along the shore.

SEEN IT?

MY DRAWINGS AND PHOTOS

Ringed plover *Charadrius hiaticula*

S hort and stocky, ringed plovers are small wading birds that usually gather in large flocks, especially at high tide. They have obvious black markings next to their white feathers. This bold pattern helps the birds to blend in against shingle and pebbles on the beach.

SIZE 18–20 cm

WINGSPAN 48–58 cm

CALL 'Too-li'

HABITAT Sandy beaches, shingle shores and inland gravel pits

BREEDING 2–3 eggs from April to August

white stripe just above eye

bill is short with orange-and-black bands

sandy-coloured feathers on back

dark band across breast

orange legs

camouflaged eggs

I saw this bird in: Spring ○ Summer ○ Autumn ○ Winter ○

MY OBSERVATIONS

Location: _____

Time: _____

The weather is: _____

_____

How many can I see? _____

_____

What is it/are they doing? _____

_____

_____

_____

Shelducks usually lay their nests on the ground. Adults birds often look after chicks that are not their own.

SEEN IT?

MY DRAWINGS AND PHOTOS

Shelduck *Tadorna tadorna*

Although some shelducks live inland, most live in coastal habitats and can be seen all year round. These large ducks have a call similar to that of some geese. Shelducks wade through shallow water, sweeping their bills from side to side as they hunt for animals such as crustaceans to eat. They also graze on seaweed.

SIZE 60–70 cm

WINGSPAN 110–130 cm

CALL Males call 'huee', females call 'ak-ak-ak'

HABITAT Sandy and muddy shores, estuaries

BREEDING 8–10 eggs laid February to August

dark green-black head

bright red bill with knob above nostrils

mostly white plumage

rusty-coloured band on chest

green flash

pink legs

I saw this bird in: Spring O Summer O Autumn O Winter O

About The Wildlife Trusts

The Wildlife Trusts are committed to conserving local wildlife. There are 47 individual Wildlife Trusts covering every part of the UK, the Isle of Man and Alderney – which means there will be one near you, wherever you live.

We have more than 2250 nature reserves, looking after all the wildlife habitats found in the UK. They are fantastic places for you and your family to explore and enjoy local wildlife.

Living Seas

We don't just protect wildlife on land – we look after marine life, too. Wildlife Trusts around the UK have helped raise awareness of dolphin protection, monitored basking sharks numbers, organised underwater wildlife surveys and successfully campaigned for new laws to help protect our ocean life. Every year we run events around the UK celebrating our seas and the animals and plants that depend on them – from rockpool rambles to underwater snorkel trails. Go to www.wildlifewatch.org.uk/livingseas to find out more.

Wildlife Watch

If you're aged 5–15 and want to find out more about your local wildlife then Wildlife Watch is for you. Members receive a welcome pack, a wildlife magazine and poster four times a year – and access to local events and activities! Go to www.wildlifewatch.org.uk/membership for more information.

Discover your local wildlife!